RUTH
BADER
GINSBURG

RUTH BADER

GINSBURG

BY CHRISTOPHER HENRY

A FIRST BOOK

FRANKLIN WATTS

New York / Chicago / London / Toronto / Sydney

Cover photograph copyright ©: Archive Photos; Supreme Court
Historical Society (inset)

Photographs copyright ©: Smithsonian Institution/Richard W. Strauss: pp. 2, 56;
AP/Wide World Photos: pp. 6, 14, 20, 24, 29, 32, 41, 44, 45, 46, 51, 54; The
Bettmann Archive: pp. 12, 26; New York Public Library, Picture Collection: p. 16;
Archive Photos, NYC: pp. 18, 39; The Brooklyn Historical Society: p. 23; Harvard Law
School Yearbook: p. 31; Columbia University School of Law: pp. 34, 42; Rutgers Law
School, Newark: p. 36; Jay Mallin: pp. 48, 53.

Library of Congress Cataloging-in-Publication Data

Henry, Christopher E.
    Ruth Bader Ginsburg / Christopher E. Henry
        p. cm. — (First book)
    Includes bibliographical references and index.
        ISBN 0-531-20174-0
    1. Ginsburg, Ruth Bader—Juvenile literature. 2. Judges—United States—Biography—
Juvenile literature. [1. Ginsburg, Ruth Bader. 2. United States. Supreme Court—
    Biography. 3. Judges. 4. Women—Biography.] I. Title. II. Series.
            KF8745.G56H46 1994
            347.73'2634—dc20
                [B]
            [347.3073534]
        [B]   94-978 CIP AC

For Paul O'Dwyer, Esq. — statesman, author,
and noted civil rights lawyer — who has inspired so
many of his colleagues to defend those without power
and to speak for those with no voice.

With friendship and respect.

To my mother, Celia Amster Bader, the bravest, strongest person I have known, who was taken from me much too soon. I pray that I may be all that she would have been, had she lived in an age when women could aspire and achieve, and daughters are cherished as much as sons.

U.S. Circuit Judge Ruth Bader Ginsburg's remarks at the White House after her nomination to the U.S. Supreme Court, June 14, 1993

CONTENTS

RUTH
BADER
GINSBURG

The Bader family, along with many other first- and second-generation immigrant families, made their home in bustling Brooklyn.

CHAPTER 1

THE DREAMS OF IMMIGRANTS

On March 15, 1933, in the Brooklyn neighborhood known as Flatbush, Celia and Nathan Bader became the proud parents of their second child, whom they named Ruth. They were happy that their older daughter, Marilyn, would now have a playmate and little sister. Many newly arrived immigrants lived in Flatbush then. Although Celia and Nathan had been born in the United States, their parents were Russian and eastern European Jews who had come to America seeking a better life and freedom from religious persecution.

Brooklyn, one of the five counties, or "boroughs," that make up New York City, was home to almost a hundred different nationalities, races, and religions. Although most of the people in Brooklyn did their best to get along with each other and live peacefully, there was still a great deal of prejudice. Some neighborhoods were unsafe for Jews to enter, while others were dangerous for African Americans or Irish or Greeks.

*Celia Amster Bader taught her daughter
the importance of hard work, achievement,
and, above all, education.*

As with other children of her faith in Brooklyn, Ruth Bader learned, at a very early age, what it meant to be a Jew. Her parents taught her the history of her people and told her of the suffering and sacrifice that had brought their families to America. Ruth's daily experiences taught her that anti-Jewish bigotry did not magically stop at *Ellis Island*. As a little girl, Ruth Bader Ginsburg read signs on storefronts proclaiming "No Jews Allowed." *Anti-Semitism* was abundant in Brooklyn and, with other forms of discrimination, was as much a part of daily life as a ride on the subway.

Ruth's mother was, without a doubt, the single most important influence in her early life — and perhaps in her entire life. As a young girl, her mother (then Celia Amster) had been an excellent student and graduated from high school several years earlier than most of her peers. Celia had hungered for a college education and dreamed of a career. Her father, however, like many people in those days, believed that higher education was wasted on women, because they were generally expected to become wives and mothers and full-time homemakers.

So Mr. Amster sent his young daughter to work. Celia's job in New York City's garment district required long, hard hours of work. Not only was she denied the education she yearned for, but she had to contribute the money she earned to pay her brother's college tuition. Sadly, Celia watched her chances for intellectual and professional fulfillment slip away.

Like many Jewish workers of the time, Ruth's mother made clothing in the squalid factories called sweatshops in New York City's garment district.

After she married Nathan Bader, Celia's heartache grew as she realized that she would never earn a college degree or have a career of her own. She was determined to make sure that her children were not deprived of any educational opportunities. Celia's determination was reinforced by a tragedy that devastated the Bader family for years to come. Their older daughter, Marilyn, contracted meningitis and died when she was just eight years old. Suddenly, with the loss of one of her two children, Celia focused all of her love as well as all of her worries on Ruth. Sometimes the pressure on Ruth was almost unbearable, but she resolved not to disappoint her mother.

Ruth's father, Nathan Bader, was a businessman. He was smart, inventive, and hardworking but, as with many small businessmen in Depression-era America, he barely made ends meet much of the time. Nathan owned several businesses during his life, but his two chief ventures were in the clothing industry as a furrier who bought and sold fur coats, hats, and wraps, and as a haberdasher with his own store in Brooklyn. Despite a lifetime of seventy-hour workweeks, Nathan never became wealthy. During hard times, he was happy just to keep food on his family's table and pay the rent.

Celia Bader, though, maintained a certain amount of economic independence from her husband. She religiously put money aside each week, even in those tough times when Nathan lost more money than he made. Whether

In one of his business ventures, Nathan Bader ran a haberdashery (a store that sells men's clothing and accessories) similar to the one pictured here.

Nathan knew what she was doing or ever realized how much his wife had saved is uncertain. But by the time Ruth entered her last year of high school, her mother had amassed enough money to send her to college.

Celia had also made sure that her daughter would be prepared academically. She pushed Ruth to read as much as she could and above all to excel at her academic studies. When Ruth was still in grammar school, Celia would take her to the public library, where they would spend hours together reading and discussing their favorite books. Not only did Celia fill her daughter with a love of learning but in Ruth's mind, learning and reading became inseparably connected with her mother's love and approval.

There were, of course, conflicts between Ruth and her mother about how hard she would study and how she would choose to live her life. She did not simply accept her mother's plans without raising serious questions and objections.

At times Ruth Bader seemed caught between two worlds. Her grandparents had fled Europe and Russia, risking their lives so that their children would know the benefits of life in America. Her parents had worked day and night to make a new life for the family in Brooklyn and to provide the material necessities and conveniences that made life enjoyable. However, as a third-generation American, Ruth could never fully understand the desperation of her grandparents or the burning ambitions of her mother and father.

Like many teenagers, Ruth struggled to be independent of her parents and make her own decisions.

CHAPTER 2

CELIA BADER'S LEGACY

Although Ruth Bader was always serious about her schoolwork, she had many interests unrelated to academics. Ruth was a cheerleader and baton twirler, an accomplished musician who played the cello in the school orchestra, and one of the editors of the *Moment*, James Madison High School's student newspaper. She was also well liked and pretty.

Despite all of her activities, sense of humor, and personal popularity, Ruth carried a heavy burden. She was reminded each day of her sister's death, more by her mother's concern than by anything she said. The message was clear: Ruth alone could fulfill her mother's hopes.

Celia Bader had a far greater influence on her young daughter than simply inspiring her to achieve and succeed. She was a woman of high moral values and ideals, which she taught to Ruth as well. Celia deeply believed in the worth of every human life and was dedicated to one overriding principle — that all people should be treated with fairness and respect, regardless of their economic status, race, religion, or gender. She provided her daughter with a moral foundation that did more than assure Ruth's future professional success. Ruth was also assured of making a personal contribution to society, and helping others, particularly women, to achieve and succeed in America.

When Ruth was in her first year of high school, Celia Bader was stricken with cervical cancer. Her health gradually deteriorated during the next few years. All through high school, Ruth attempted to lead a "normal" academic and social life, never wanting Celia to know how much anguish her illness caused her. She wanted to prove to her mother that everything was all right and would be all right in the future. Ruth realized that Celia was, in her last years, living her own unfulfilled dreams through her daughter.

In Ruth's senior year, Celia Bader's condition worsened, and she would often spend long periods of each day in bed, and then entire days, and then several days in a row. Her strength was ebbing, and perhaps her will to live was dimming as well. Celia knew, from Ruth's report cards, that her most important mission in life had been accomplished: her daughter would have a college education and all of the opportunities that went along with it.

In June 1950, on the night before Ruth's graduation from James Madison High School, Celia Amster Bader died at the age of forty-seven. For more than three years,

During her mother's illness, Ruth
found comfort in the daily routine of life at
James Madison High School in Brooklyn.

Although she posed for her senior yearbook picture in graduation robes, Ruth did not attend her high school graduation.

she had fought cancer as she watched her daughter grow into a woman of substance.

Ruth must have been overwhelmed by her mother's death but also relieved that Celia's suffering had finally ended. She did not attend her graduation ceremonies but instead helped to make arrangements for her mother's funeral.

Both men and women have studied at Cornell University since 1872, when it became the first university to admit women. Here, students pass by the school library and its bell tower between classes.

CHAPTER 3

THE WORLD OUTSIDE BROOKLYN

R uth's grades in high school allowed her a wide choice of colleges. She decided on Cornell University and, in the late summer of 1950, began her studies there. Ruth was surprised to discover that the college placed her in a dormitory filled with Jewish girls from the New York City area. She hoped the housing assignments were given to allow students with shared interests to live together. She also recognized the possibility that discrimination was at work — that the university had created a kind of Jewish *ghetto*.

Ruth, however, was not discouraged easily. Her mother's recent death had intensified her determination to succeed, and as a full-scholarship student at Cornell, she had to justify the financial aid she received. Ruth was an excellent student. When she received her bachelor of arts degree from Cornell in the spring of 1954 she was, once again, near the top of her class.

Shortly after she arrived at Cornell University, Ruth met a young man named Martin Ginsburg. Martin's roommate was dating one of Ruth's friends at Cornell. On a hunch that Martin might be a suitable match for the studious and somewhat reserved Ruth, the friends talked them into going on a blind date.

On the surface, Martin was very different from Ruth. A year ahead of her in school, he came from a much wealthier background and had grown up on Long Island. Martin's family had not experienced the financial difficulties or family tragedies that Ruth's family had endured. With plenty of spending money, his own car, and an outstanding golfing record at Cornell, Martin was relaxed and confident about the future. Although the two may have been equally ambitious, Martin was more carefree and far less intimidated by life than Ruth. They complemented each other perfectly.

After he graduated from college in 1953, Martin began his graduate studies at Harvard Law School. By this time, Ruth and he had already made plans to marry immediately after her graduation from Cornell. Their relationship continued through phone calls, letters, and weekend and holiday visits. But a few months before he completed his first year at Harvard, something unexpected happened — he was drafted into the U.S. Army.

Ruth and Martin were married, as planned, in June 1954, shortly after she graduated from Cornell. Although Ruth had been planning to attend law school after graduation, possibly at Harvard with her husband, she began her married life as an army wife instead.

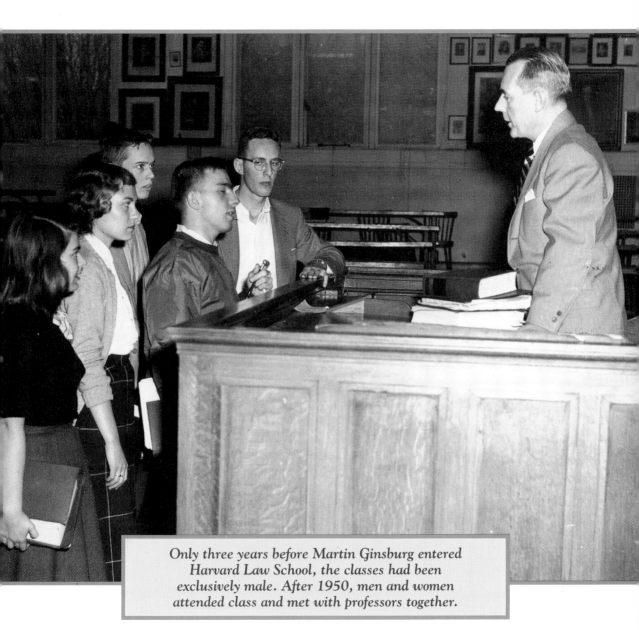

Only three years before Martin Ginsburg entered Harvard Law School, the classes had been exclusively male. After 1950, men and women attended class and met with professors together.

Martin's orders sent him to Fort Sill, Oklahoma, which is one of the U.S. Army's major training and administrative centers. Fort Sill is more than 1,000 miles (1,600 km) from Brooklyn, but for Ruth and Martin Ginsburg, it might as well have been light-years away from Brooklyn or Long Island. They remained at Fort Sill for the next two years.

Ruth did her best to be a loving and supportive wife, but it wasn't easy; paying the day-to-day bills was nearly impossible on a young soldier's paycheck. She was only twenty-one years old when they had married, and although she had taken on a lot of family responsibilities during her mother's illness and after her death, Ruth's new life at Fort Sill was almost more than she had bargained for. She looked for work on the army base, but even with a degree from one of the country's best colleges, she found that opportunities were extremely limited. Very few jobs were offered to women, and they usually paid far less than the same or similar jobs held by men. Ruth finally found a government job as a clerk-typist.

Four months after she and Martin were married, Ruth became pregnant. The Ginsburgs' first child, Jane Carol, was born in July 1955. Some months before her daughter's birth, Ruth had tried to transfer into a more interesting and better paying job. When her supervisor found out that she was pregnant, he refused the promotion because, he reasoned, a pregnant woman would soon leave the workforce to become a full-time mother.

After two years in Oklahoma, Martin and Ruth Ginsburg returned east to Cambridge, Massachusetts, and law school. These photos are from the Harvard Law School yearbook.

Ruth studied law at Harvard, where this photo was taken in 1957, finally receiving her law degree from Columbia University in 1959.

Finally, two years later, Martin's hitch in the army came to an end, and the young family was able to return home. He resumed his studies at Harvard Law School, and Ruth began hers there also. It was a wonderful time for them, especially after two years on an army base in Oklahoma. Before his graduation in 1958, Martin was offered a job with a law firm in New York, which came as no surprise to the Ginsburgs. They had known all along that they would return to the New York area to live. The move, however, did force Ruth to make a sacrifice. To keep her family together, she left Harvard Law School and completed the last year of her studies in New York City. The Columbia School of Law was good but not equal in reputation to Harvard. Although she was extremely serious about her studies, Ruth Bader Ginsburg always put her family first.

During the 1950s, law classes at Columbia
were held in Kent Hall. The building
now houses the Asian Studies Library.

CHAPTER 4

A WOMAN WHO CHANGED HISTORY

Ruth Bader Ginsburg earned many honors during her academic career. She had the highest grades of any woman in her class at Cornell University and graduated as a member of Phi Beta Kappa, an honorary fraternity for outstanding academic performance. She served on the staff of both the *Harvard* and *Columbia Law Reviews*, prestigious legal journals whose membership is limited to the schools' top students.

After graduating from Columbia in 1959, she was a *clerk* for two years for a federal judge in New York City. Clerking for a federal judge is both a great honor and a great deal of work; it often leads to important career opportunities. For example, the current *chief justice* of the U.S. Supreme Court, William H. Rehnquist, began his legal career as a clerk at that court. Twenty years later, he returned as an *associate justice*.

After her judicial clerkship ended, Ruth Bader Ginsburg returned to Columbia Law School to study and

Ruth Bader Ginsburg, shown here working in her office at Rutgers University, became a full professor of law in just six years.

write about legal procedures in other parts of the world. She became an expert in Swedish law and wrote two books on the subject with another lawyer. In 1963 she finished her work at Columbia and joined the faculty at Rutgers School of Law as an assistant professor. Three years later she was promoted to the post of associate professor, and in 1969 she was named a full professor. Ruth Bader Ginsburg's rapid rise in the academic world was an extraordinary achievement.

In 1965, while she was teaching at Rutgers, the young law professor had taken a short leave to give birth to her second child, James Steven. By 1972 Ruth had returned to Columbia yet again, this time to assume a professorship at the school that had granted her a law degree. She remained there until 1980. In addition to being a full-time wife, mother, and professor of law, Ginsburg also gained prominence and some fame as a practicing attorney.

She was perhaps best known for her voluntary services to the American Civil Liberties Union (ACLU), an organization of lawyers dedicated to defending individual liberties. From 1972 until 1980, Ginsburg acted as counsel to the ACLU's Women's Rights Project. She and other lawyers from the ACLU represented clients, usually poor women who could not afford an attorney, for free. Most of the cases that they brought to the U.S. Supreme Court involved some sort of overt discrimination against women. Other cases concerned more personal matters, such as women's reproductive rights.

Ruth Bader Ginsburg's first contact with the Supreme Court came in 1971, in the case of *Reed v. Reed.* The case involved a challenge to the laws of Idaho, which gave advantages to men solely because of their sex. The facts of the case were very simple. A child named Richard Reed had died in 1967. His parents, who were legally separated, each asked for an Idaho court's permission to be the administrator of the boy's estate. The Idaho court, following the state laws, awarded the position to Richard's father. It did not matter to the court that his mother may have been just as qualified, or even more qualified, than his father. The laws of Idaho gave preference to males in such matters.

Ginsburg and several other attorneys wrote the *briefs,* or arguments, that were presented to the Supreme Court. The written argument is usually much more important than any *oral argument* made before the Court, because the Supreme Court does not conduct trials. With a very few exceptions, the U.S. Supreme Court only reviews the actions of other, "inferior" courts, to determine if those courts properly applied the law and correctly interpreted the U.S. Constitution.

There are nine *justices* on the Supreme Court, and all of them voted to overturn the Idaho law, which they said illegally discriminated against women. The decision of the Court in *Reed v. Reed* represented not only a tremendous personal victory for Ginsburg, but also for women's rights activists all over the country.

The inscription above the columns of the Supreme Court
Building in Washington, D.C., guarantees
"equal justice under law."

Two years later, Ruth Bader Ginsburg made her first oral argument before the Supreme Court appearing before the justices and answering their questions about a case known as *Frontiero v. Richardson*. Sharron Frontiero, a female officer of the U.S. Air Force, had been denied housing and medical benefits for her husband. Those same benefits were automatically granted to male Air Force officers for their wives. The benefits were denied because Frontiero was a woman, and the Air Force readily admitted this to be the case.

The Supreme Court's decision — in favor of Sharron Frontiero and against the U.S. Air Force — was not unanimous, but it was overwhelming. Eight of the nine justices voted in Sharron Frontiero's favor, finding that the Air Force's regulations violated the *due process clause* of the Fifth Amendment to the Constitution. Only Justice Rehnquist dissented. Ginsburg had helped to win an enormous victory for women as well as for their husbands.

One of the reasons Ruth Bader Ginsburg was so successful before the Supreme Court was her commonsense approach to the practice of law. Because all of the justices on the Court were men, Ginsburg knew that it would be easier to "sell" arguments in cases that involved men's as well as women's rights. Ruth's mother may have been her greatest influence and inspiration, but she had learned a lot about selling from her father and his business. The *Frontiero* case was a perfect example of this approach

When Ginsburg wrote the briefs for a 1971 Supreme Court case, the justices were all male and, except for Associate Justice Thurgood Marshall (standing far left), all white.

because although Sharron Frontiero was a woman seeking benefits based on her own military status and rank, they were benefits for her husband.

Several cases that Ruth Bader Ginsburg helped to bring before the U.S. Supreme Court in the following years

This class on gender discrimination was among
the many courses Professor Ginsburg taught
at the Columbia University School of Law.

involved getting men rights traditionally reserved for women. Ginsburg proved herself to be the fairest of individuals. She was just as willing to fight for the rights of a man as for those of a woman. In Ginsburg's mind, both men and women lost out when laws discriminated based on sex. Because of her insight and evenhandedness, Ruth Bader Ginsburg became perhaps the most famous advocate of equal rights — for women *and* men — in the history of the United States.

Perhaps the case that best demonstrates Ruth Bader Ginsburg's values and beliefs in regard to discrimination based on sex is *Califano v. Goldfarb*, which was decided in 1977. Once again Ginsburg was chosen to present the oral argument to the Supreme Court. She represented Mr. Goldfarb, whose wife had died in 1968. Mr. Goldfarb, as a widower, was denied certain Social Security benefits that widows routinely received. Thus Ginsburg was again presenting a case that affected the rights of both women and men. The Social Security Administration denied women the right to leave survivors' benefits to their husbands and denied surviving husbands their right to receive those benefits.

As usual, Ginsburg was victorious, but this time by the barest of margins. Five of the nine Supreme Court justices agreed with her that the Social Security regulation was *unconstitutional*; the other four justices voted to uphold the regulation.

In 1978, Ruth Bader Ginsburg visited
daughter Jane at Harvard. Jane followed
family tradition by studying law there.

Throughout their marriage, Ruth and Martin Ginsburg have been supportive of one another's careers.

The last time that Ruth Bader Ginsburg appeared before the Supreme Court, she argued on behalf of the rights of a man whom very few people could like. The case was *Duren v. Missouri*, and it challenged a Missouri law that allowed women but not men to be excused from *jury duty* at their own request.

Mr. Duren had been convicted of robbery and murder,

From the time she entered law school as the mother of a young child, Ruth Bader Ginsburg has successfully balanced her professional and family responsibilities. From left are her son-in-law, George Spera, daughter Jane, husband Martin, and son James. In front are George and Jane's children, Clara and Paul.

but claimed that he might not have been convicted if the *jury* at his trial had been composed of men and women in roughly equal numbers. No women sat on the jury that had convicted Mr. Duren. He alleged that male jurors were less sympathetic and more willing to vote for conviction than were female jurors.

Ginsburg based her oral arguments on the *Sixth Amendment* of the U.S. Constitution, which guarantees "an impartial jury of the State and district wherein the crime shall have been committed." Ginsburg argued that a jury-selection system that resulted in juries that were made up only, or mostly, of men violated the Sixth Amendment.

The case, decided by the Supreme Court in 1979, provided a final and fitting victory for Ruth Bader Ginsburg as an advocate before the Court. The Court voted to invalidate Mr. Duren's conviction and ruled that the Missouri laws were unconstitutional. Eight of the nine Supreme Court justices joined in the decision. Once again, Justice Rehnquist was the sole dissenter. That Ruth Bader Ginsburg willingly and successfully argued a case defending the rights of a convicted criminal is a tribute both to her integrity and to her legal skill.

*In 1980, Judge Ruth Bader Ginsburg took
her seat on the U.S. Court of Appeals
for the District of Columbia.*

CHAPTER 5

JUSTICE
GINSBURG

I n 1980, near the end of his term in office, President Jimmy Carter appointed Ruth Bader Ginsburg to the federal bench. After being confirmed by the U.S. Senate, she became a *circuit judge* of the *U.S. Court of Appeals* for the District of Columbia. The Court of Appeals is the second-highest level of the federal court system — only the Supreme Court can reverse the rulings of the Court of Appeals.

As Judge Ruth Bader Ginsburg, she was, at the age of forty-seven, faced with an entirely new challenge. No longer an advocate who argues and fights for justice for individuals, Judge Ginsburg was now called on to interpret the laws and the Constitution objectively. Instead of representing the interests of individual clients, she now represented the laws of the nation and was sworn to do so, even if she personally disagreed with those laws.

Those who knew her best and had worked with her in the previous decade expected Ruth Bader Ginsburg to be an *activist judge*. Activist judges believe that their responsibilities do not end with the simple, limited interpretation of the law. They feel that the courts and the decisions offered by them should provide broad directions and assistance to the *legislature* in the lawmaking process.

Judge Ginsburg proved her colleagues correct in her first year on the bench. In *Wright v. Regan*, the parents of black children claimed that private schools that discriminated on the basis of race in their admission policies had unlawfully been exempted from paying taxes. In this case, Judge Ginsburg showed her judicial activism by voting to overturn a lower court's decision to deny the parents the right to bring the action.

Ruth Bader Ginsburg served on the Court of Appeals for thirteen years, and her opinions demonstrated not only a brilliant legal mind but a sincere compassion for those affected by her decisions. Then in 1993, Justice Byron White announced his retirement from the Supreme Court. Bill Clinton, elected the nation's forty-second president the year before, considered numerous possible nominees for the Supreme Court seat. Some presidents, such as Jimmy Carter, never had the opportunity to appoint a Supreme Court justice. In fact, President Clinton was the first Democratic president in more than a quarter-century to do so; it would be one of the most important decisions of Clinton's political career. After weeks of speculation, he nominated Ruth Bader Ginsburg to the nation's highest court.

President Bill Clinton applauds his Supreme Court nominee in the Rose Garden at the White House. Judge Ginsburg wore her mother's circle pin, as she had for all six of her oral arguments before the Supreme Court.

Ginsburg became the second woman ever nominated to the Supreme Court. The first, Judge Sandra Day O'Connor, was nominated in 1981 by President Ronald Reagan and then confirmed to the Court by the Senate. With Judge Ginsburg's nomination, it was possible that for the first time in history the Supreme Court would have two women in its ranks.

First, however, Judge Ginsburg would have to be approved by the Senate. During her testimony before the Senate Judiciary Committee, there was much speculation in the press about Ginsburg's political philosophy. She was asked numerous questions about her views on the role of the Court in the making of laws.

Ginsburg's writings offered some clues to her outlook. She praised those members of the federal judiciary who were neither liberal nor conservative, but "independent-thinking" individuals who were "skeptical of all party lines." These were the judges whom Ginsburg sought to follow, she stated. There had been many bitter confirmation battles in the Senate, especially in the previous two decades. Several nominees' names had been withdrawn from consideration and others approved by narrow margins or rejected outright, but Ginsburg was confirmed easily — virtually without objection.

On August 10, 1993, a warm, sunny day, with President Clinton by her side, Ruth Bader Ginsburg was sworn into office by Chief Justice Rehnquist at an outdoor cere-

During her Senate confirmation hearing, Ruth Bader Ginsburg impressed the Judiciary Committee and others with her measured, thoughtful responses.

Supreme Court Justice Ruth Bader Ginsburg takes the oath to defend the Constitution from Chief Justice William Rehnquist in the East Room of the White House. Martin Ginsburg holds the Bible as President Clinton looks on.

mony at the White House. In her acceptance speech, she spoke of the sacrifices of the thousands of women who had lived in times when such accomplishments were impossible. In particular, Justice Ginsburg paid tribute to her mother, Celia Amster Bader, a woman whose own dreams had been denied but whose hopes and sacrifices for her daughter would one day be remembered as part of American history.

The Supreme Court, 1993
(clockwise from upper left) Associate Justices Clarence
Thomas, Anthony M. Kennedy, David H. Souter, Ruth
Bader Ginsburg, Antonin Scalia, and John Paul Stevens,
Chief Justice William H. Rehnquist, and Associate Justices
Harry A. Blackmun and Sandra Day O'Connor.

GLOSSARY

Activist judge — a judge who believes that courts and judges should play an active part in shaping national policies.

Anti-Semitism — dislike of or discrimination against Jews because of their religion or ethnicity.

Brief — the written summary prepared by a lawyer outlining the facts and the legal arguments of one side of a case.

Circuit judge — a judge who presides over one of thirteen regional (or circuit) courts of appeals, usually with two other judges on any particular case.

Clerk — a position of responsibility assisting a judge or justice in the preparation, research, and writing of legal opinions.

Due process clause — parts of the Fifth or Fourteenth Amendments that protect individuals from unfair treatment by the government.

Ellis Island — the island in New York Harbor where, until 1954, most new immigrants to the United States were processed.

Ghetto — sections of cities that are home to minority groups because of social, legal, or economic pressure. Originally the term referred to the part of European cities where Jews were forced to live.

Jury; jury duty — a group of citizens chosen to hear two sides of a legal argument and decide the case; the obligation to serve on a jury.

Justice (associate or chief) — one of nine judges serving on the Supreme Court who reviews mostly decisions of state courts and of lower U.S. courts. There are eight associate justices and one chief (or head) justice.

Legislature — the lawmaking branch of government.

Oral argument — a lawyer's statements made before the Court summarizing the main points of a case and responding to the justices' questions.

Sixth Amendment — a part of the Bill of Rights (the original ten amendments to the Constitution) that protects the right of the accused to "a speedy and public trial, by an impartial jury."

Unconstitutional — violating or inconsistent with the U.S. Constitution.

U.S. Court of Appeals — after the Supreme Court, the second highest level of the federal judicial system. Each court of appeals (there are thirteen) reviews contested rulings of cases tried in lower courts. They may uphold or reverse the decision or send the case back to the lower court for reconsideration.

FOR FURTHER READING

Aria, Barbara. *The Supreme Court*. New York: Franklin Watts, 1994.

Henry, Christopher. *Sandra Day O'Connor*. New York: Franklin Watts, 1994.

Italia, Robert. *Ruth Bader Ginsburg*. Edina, Minn.: Abdo & Daughters, 1994.

Reef, Catherine. *The Supreme Court*. New York: Dillon, 1994.

Roberts, Jack L. *Ruth Bader Ginsburg: Supreme Court Justice*. Brookfield, Conn.: Millbrook Press, 1994.

INDEX

Italicized page numbers indicate illustrations.

ABOUT THE AUTHOR

Christopher Henry is a New York attorney in private practice. He is the author of two books about American immigration law and several books for children, including biographies of Ben Nighthorse Campbell and Henry Cisneros. He has also written the Watts First Book biography *Sandra Day O'Connor*.